TULSA CITY-COUNTY LIBRARY

HRJC

JUL - - 2022

Summer Food

Julie Murray

Abdo Kids Junior
is an Imprint of Abdo Kids
abdobooks.com

Abdo
Kids
SEASONS: SUMMER SHINE!

abdobooks.com

Published by Abdo Kids, a division of ABDO, P.O. Box 398166, Minneapolis, Minnesota 55439. Copyright © 2022 by Abdo Consulting Group, Inc. International copyrights reserved in all countries. No part of this book may be reproduced in any form without written permission from the publisher. Abdo Kids Junior™ is a trademark and logo of Abdo Kids.

Printed in the United States of America, North Mankato, Minnesota.
102021
012022

THIS BOOK CONTAINS RECYCLED MATERIALS

Photo Credits: Getty Images, Shutterstock

Production Contributors: Teddy Borth, Jennie Forsberg, Grace Hansen

Design Contributors: Candice Keimig, Pakou Moua

Library of Congress Control Number: 2021940031
Publisher's Cataloging-in-Publication Data

Names: Murray, Julie, author.

Title: Summer food / by Julie Murray

Description: Minneapolis, Minnesota : Abdo Kids, 2022 | Series: Seasons: summer shine! | Includes online resources and index.

Identifiers: ISBN 9781098209322 (lib. bdg.) | ISBN 9781098260033 (ebook) | ISBN 9781098260385 (Read-to-Me ebook)

Subjects: LCSH: Summer--Juvenile literature. | Food--Juvenile literature. | Food supply--Seasonal variations--Juvenile literature. | Produce trade--Seasonal variations--Juvenile literature. | Seasons--Juvenile literature.

Classification: DDC 525.5--dc23

Table of Contents

Summer Food 4

More
Summer Food 22

Glossary 23

Index 24

Abdo Kids Code 24

Summer Food

Summer is here! It's time for something **refreshing**.

The peaches are **ripe**.

Tara picks them.

Val takes a bite of watermelon. It is juicy!

Tia cuts the cucumber.

She adds it to her salad.

Mia eats ice cream with her friends.

12

Matt **gathers** blackberries.

He fills up a bowl.

Lee is in his garden.

He picks tomatoes.

Sam loves to eat corn on the cob.

What summer food do you like to eat?

More Summer Food

blueberries

broccoli

cantaloupe

raspberries

Glossary

gather
to collect and bring together into one place.

refreshing
making you feel more rested, energetic, cool, etc. after you have felt tired or hot.

ripe
fully grown and ready for eating.

Index

blackberry 14

corn 18

cucumber 10

ice cream 12

peach 6

salad 10

tomato 16

watermelon 8

Visit **abdokids.com** to access crafts, games, videos, and more!

Use Abdo Kids code **SSK9322** or scan this QR code!